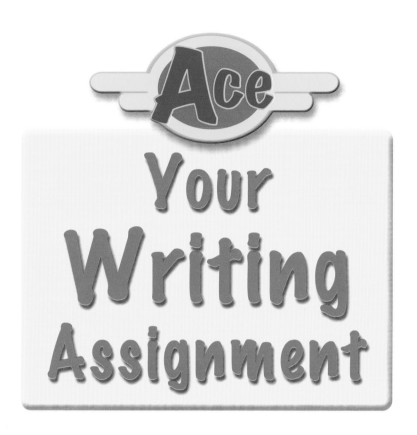

Your Writing Assignment

by Dana Meachen Rau

Enslow Elementary

an imprint of

Enslow Publishers, Inc.

40 Industrial Road
Box 398
Berkeley Heights, NJ 07922
USA

http://www.enslow.com

The author would like to thank Kelly Sanders, Literacy Specialist, West District School, Farmington, Connecticut, and Christie Wall, Third-Grade Teacher, Lake Garda School, Burlington, Connecticut, for the helpful conversations during the writing of this book.

Enslow Elementary, an imprint of Enslow Publishers, Inc.

Enslow Elementary® is a registered trademark of Enslow Publishers, Inc.

Library of Congress Cataloging-in-Publication Data
Rau, Dana Meachen, 1971–
  Ace your writing assignment / Dana Meachen Rau.
    p. cm. — (Ace it! information literacy series)
  Includes bibliographical references and index.
  Summary: "Learn how to make your writing better and more interesting"—Provided by publisher.
  ISBN-13: 978-0-7660-3394-8
  ISBN-10: 0-7660-3394-5
  1. Composition (Language arts)—Juvenile literature. 2. English language—Composition and exercises—Juvenile literature. I. Title.
  LB1576.R373 2009
  372.62'3—dc22
                              2008024887

Printed in the United States of America

10 9 8 7 6 5 4 3 2 1

To Our Readers:
We have done our best to make sure all Internet Addresses in this book were active and appropriate when we went to press. However, the author and the publisher have no control over and assume no liability for the material available on those Internet sites or on other Web sites they may link to. Any comments or suggestions can be sent by e-mail to comments@enslow.com or to the address on the back cover.

♻ Enslow Publishers, Inc., is committed to printing our books on recycled paper. The paper in every book contains 10% to 30% post-consumer waste (PCW). The cover board on the outside of each book contains 100% PCW. Our goal is to do our part to help young people and the environment too!

Cover photo: Corbis/Kevin Dodge
Interior photos: Corbis/Noel Hendrickson, p. 10; Getty Images/Wides & Holl/Taxi, p. 34; The Image Works/Jeff Greenberg, p. 4; The Image Works/Jacksonville Journal Courier, p. 18; The Image Works/Bob Daemmrich, p. 32; iStockphoto.com/Andres Peiro, pp. 3, 5, 11, 19, 25, 33, 37, 39; iStockphoto.com/Emrah Turudu, pp. 7, 31, 32; iStockphoto.com/Mustafa Deliormanli, p. 23; iStockphoto.com/YinYang, p. 26; iStockphoto.com/Wolfgang Steiner, p. 29; iStockphoto.com/Brad Shockley, p. 36; Jupiter Images/Comstock, p. 16; Jupiter Images/Christina Kennedy/Brand X Pictures, p. 9; Photo Edit/Michael Newman, p. 24; Photo Edit/David Young-Wolff, p. 38; Photo Researchers, Inc./Eunice Harris, p. 20; Photolibrary/Darren Greenwood, p. 6; Photolibrary/Radius Images, p. 13; Photolibrary/JDC, LWA, p. 42.

Contents

It takes a lot of hard work to build an ice cream shop. Writing is challenging, too—but the rewards are sweet!

Building with Words

Have you ever dreamed of opening an ice cream shop? Imagine streams of eager customers lined up to buy your ice cream. Imagine the buckets of colorful flavors. Imagine being surrounded by ice cream morning, noon, and night!

You can't just wake up one day and start selling ice cream, though. You have to build a shop first. Building is a process with many steps. It takes time, patience, and hard work.

Writing is like building an ice cream shop. When you write, you need to follow a process, too. At the end

Writing Steps

Step 1: Prewriting

Step 2: Drafting

Step 3: Revision

Step 4: Peer Review

Step 5: Publishing

5

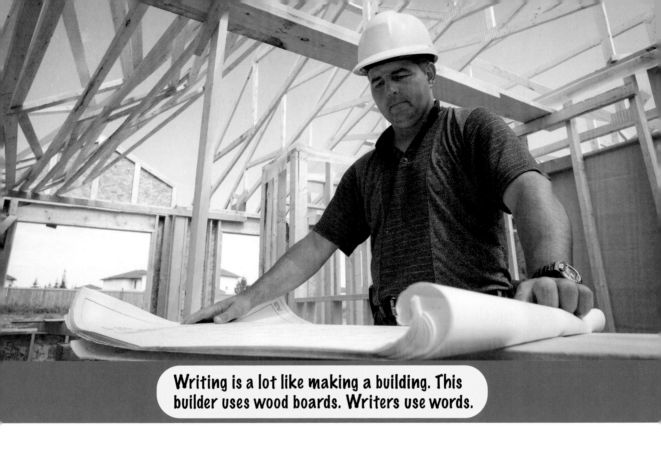

Writing is a lot like making a building. This builder uses wood boards. Writers use words.

you'll have a great piece of writing to share. The writing process includes five main steps.

Step 1: Prewriting

The builder of an ice cream shop has to create a blueprint. A blueprint is a plan for a building. You should also make a blueprint when you write. Prewriting means getting prepared to write. You organize your thoughts in a way that makes sense.

Step 2: Drafting

As she follows her blueprint, a builder puts up walls of wood and brick. You need to build walls, too. A writer's walls are made up of words and paragraphs. Putting the words on paper is called drafting.

Step 3: Revision

The walls of the ice cream shop are up! But there are still fixes to make. A builder makes sure everything is just right—all the way down to the flavors of ice cream. Your writing needs fixing, too. It also needs flavor. A writer's flavors are the details that make a topic tasty for the reader. Adding flavor is called revision.

Step 4: Peer Review

A builder's work has one last step. He needs to call in an inspector. An inspector checks to make sure the building is safe and well built. A peer review is when you let other kids read your work. They give you feedback. Your friend or classmate is your inspector. His or her opinions can help

The Writing Tool Belt

You don't need too many tools to start writing. You just need a pen and paper or a computer.

Computers come with special tools that make drafting and revising easier. In word-processing programs, you can easily take out and add words. You can move words and paragraphs from one place to another. You can insert pictures, make the size of words bigger, and even check your spelling.

improve your writing. Your peer reviewer will find mistakes that you missed.

Step 5: Publishing

The shop is done! It's time to sell ice cream to customers. As a writer, your shop is open when your work is finished. Then you can share your piece with readers. Publishing is a way to share your writing in its best possible form.

A builder starts with a plot of land. You can start with a blank piece of paper. Pick up your tools and get ready for some work!

Kinds of Writing

Expository—for Information	Creative—for Entertainment
book report	personal narrative (story about your own life)
science report	fiction story
history report	play
how-to instructions	poem
thank-you note	comic book
compare and contrast essay	song
opinion piece	myth

The writing journey begins with a blank piece of paper—or a blank computer screen.

The building process starts with a drawing called a blueprint. When you write, you will also create a blueprint.

Making the Blueprint: Prewriting

Should an ice cream shop have lots of windows? Should it be three stories high, or just one? Should it have booths or seats at a counter? Builders have many choices to make before they start nailing boards or laying bricks. Writers start by asking themselves questions, too. This is part of **Step 1: Prewriting**.

Why am I writing this?

Ask yourself why you are writing in the first place. Then you will know where to start. If your answer is "to have fun," then your piece is probably creative writing. If your answer is "to share information" or "to teach my reader something," then your

Step 1: Prewriting

Step 2: Drafting

Step 3: Revision

Step 4: Peer Review

Step 5: Publishing

piece is expository writing. Expository writing describes something, lists facts, or compares things. It can also give an opinion. For expository writing, you might have to do some research. Research is hunting for information about your topic.

Plagiarism

When you do research, you will discover some great ideas. You might want to put someone else's words or pictures in your own work. If you do this, you must give the name of the person who did the work. Plagiarism is pretending someone else's work is your own. It is against your school rules. If you plagiarize, you could get a zero on your assignment. In college, you could get kicked out of school.

Who is my reader?

Is your piece an assignment from your teacher? Is it a story to show your classmates? Is it a letter to a friend? Think about your reader. This will help you decide what to include. A teacher might give you a rubric to get you started. A rubric is like a checklist. It tells you what your teacher expects from your writing.

What is my main idea?

The main idea is what your piece will be about. Try to be specific about your main idea. "Autumn" is a broad idea. "Sports to play in autumn" is more specific.

What are my supporting details?

Supporting details are small facts and ideas. They support, or help tell about, your main idea. Let's say your main idea is "Sports to play in autumn." Your supporting details could be "soccer, football, and field hockey."

Now that you have done some thinking and researching, you can make a blueprint. Writers sometimes use graphic organizers to make a blueprint. A graphic organizer is your writing plan.

You can always ask your teacher for help with a writing assignment.

13

A Brain Storm!

Some writers get started by brainstorming. A real storm can be messy. Leaves blow, lightning flashes, and waves crash on a shore. A brainstorm can be messy, too. Brainstorming is making a list of everything that pops into your head. Usually you start by writing down your topic. Then you make a list of ideas. The list doesn't have to be organized. You can even brainstorm by drawing pictures! Brainstorming works really well with a writing partner or group.

You don't even need to use complete sentences. Just jot down your ideas. Third-grade teacher Christie Wall of Burlington, Connecticut, tells her students, "Using a graphic organizer is like using a map on a long trip. You think about where you are going and then plan the routes so that you get to your destination."[1]

A Venn diagram is a helpful graphic organizer. It helps you compare and contrast two people or things. You think about how they are alike and different. The Venn diagram on the next page compares and contrasts two kids named Charlie and Allie.

Venn Diagram

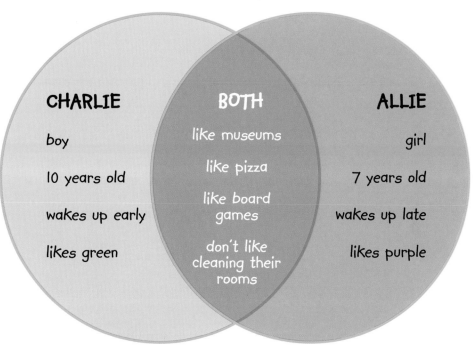

A 5 W chart asks important questions. It works well for both expository and creative writing. This graphic organizer helps you come up with basic details about the topics and people in your piece.

5 W Chart

Who?	my cat Honey
What?	liked to eat cantaloupe
When?	when she was a kitten
Where?	on the kitchen counter
Why?	because cantaloupe is sweet

A sequence chart is helpful when you want to tell events in order.

Sequence Chart

| First, | monarch butterfly lays egg |

| Next, | caterpillar hatches from egg |

| Then, | caterpillar eats milkweed leaves |

| Next, | caterpillar sheds skin and grows |

| After that, | caterpillar forms chrysalis |

| Last, | butterfly hatches from chrysalis |

Online Safety

For your writing assignment, you might have to do research on the Internet. Always get help from an adult. Visit Web sites that are safe for kids. If a site asks for information about you (such as your name, age, address, or photograph), go to another site. Never go to see someone you meet online. If a Web site makes you feel uncomfortable, close the window right away.

Word webs look a lot like blueprints. On the blueprint of an ice cream shop, you might see boxes that show rooms, counters, and tables. Your word web has boxes, too. The main idea is in the center box. Lines come out from the center to more boxes. These boxes hold your supporting details. Each supporting detail needs facts to support it, too. These come off from each supporting detail box.

Word Web

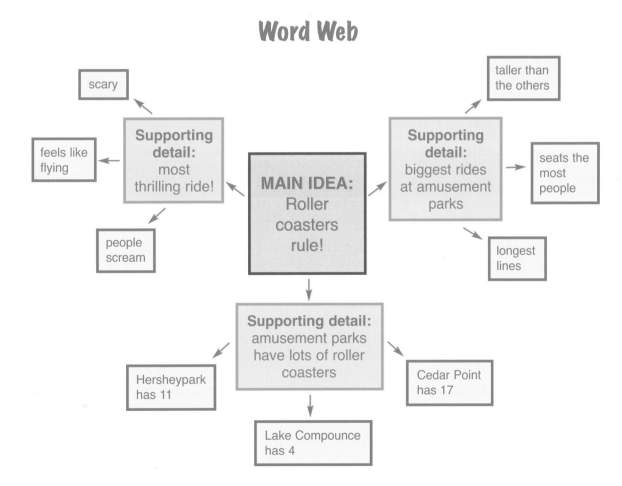

Your blueprint is finished. Now you can start laying the bricks. This is called drafting.

Laying the Bricks: Drafting

Now you have a blueprint! You can start building your piece of writing. Let's move on to **Step 2: Drafting**.

Imagine that a truck pulls up to the site where you're building your ice cream shop. It dumps out a huge pile of bricks. Now, pretend each brick is a word. A pile this big is confusing! Which words should you use? Your blueprint is your plan, and your bricks are your words. These words can be nouns, verbs, adverbs, and other kinds of words. (See Chapter 6.) As you build sentences brick by brick, your draft starts to appear.

Step 1: Prewriting

Step 2: Drafting

Step 3: Revision

Step 4: Peer Review

Step 5: Publishing

Your words need to be organized in a certain way. In most types of writing, you need to make complete sentences. Complete sentences have a subject and a predicate. The subject is the person or thing that the sentence is about. The predicate tells what the subject is doing or how the subject is feeling.

First, take a noun brick:

Fred

And add a verb brick:

Fred cooked.

Fred is the subject, and *cooked* is the predicate—the action.

This sentence looks a bit incomplete, doesn't it? The writer needs to add another word. Some sentences have a direct object or an indirect object. A direct object is the person or thing that the verb happens *to.*

Fred cooked pudding. (*Pudding* is the direct object. Pudding is what the cooking happens *to.*)

An indirect object is the person or thing the action is being done *for.* It answers the question, "For whom?"

Fred cooked Sophia pudding. (*Sophia* is the indirect object. She is the person that the action is being done *for.*)

Now, you can add some adjectives to describe your nouns. This makes your writing snappier.

Fred cooked Sophia sticky, brown chocolate pudding.

Next, try adding a prepositional phrase. This tells the reader where the action is happening.

Fred cooked Sophia sticky, brown chocolate pudding in the kitchen.

Finally, you can add clauses at the beginning or end of the sentence. Clauses give the reader more information. You can also link two sentences together to make a compound sentence.

When he was here yesterday, Fred cooked Sophia sticky, brown chocolate pudding in the kitchen, but it splattered onto the floor.

You've organized your words into sentences. Now, organize your sentences into paragraphs. In creative writing, a new paragraph usually begins a new idea. It can also show that a character is speaking. In expository writing, a paragraph needs a topic sentence and supporting sentences. A topic sentence tells the main idea of the paragraph. Supporting sentences contain the supporting details. See the example on the next page.

The first sentence is the main idea of the paragraph. It is also the topic sentence.

The other four sentences support the main idea.

The haunted house was scary. Skeletons hung from the ceiling. They rattled when I walked by. One room was black, except for two glowing red eyes. I heard a moaning sound.

The topic sentence does not always have to be first. Look at this paragraph:

Birds chirp in the trees. Green grass pokes up through the dirt. I switch my down jacket for a light sweater. These are the signs of spring.

Here, the topic sentence is the last one in the paragraph. It tells the main idea.

Your paragraphs should also be organized in a certain way. In expository writing, your first paragraph is an introduction. You state the main idea of your whole piece of writing.

The middle paragraphs have supporting details about your main idea. Each paragraph should talk about one detail.

The last paragraph is the conclusion. You summarize what you talked about and restate your main idea.

Congratulations! You've written your first draft. You're not done, though. You can always make it better. A builder might take off his construction hat and take a break . . . but then it's back to work!

Paragraphs and Their Roles

Roller Coasters Rule!

First paragraph (introduction)

Roller coasters are the kings of an amusement park. They are the largest rides. They are also the most exciting and popular rides.

Second paragraph (supporting detail)

Roller coasters are usually the biggest rides at a park. They are taller than all the other rides. Long cars of seats fit lots of people. The lines for roller coasters are the longest. Everyone wants a turn.

Third paragraph (supporting detail)

Amusement parks have lots of roller coasters. One is never enough! Even Lake Compounce, a small New England park, has four. Hersheypark in Pennsylvania has eleven. Cedar Point in Ohio has more than any other park—seventeen!

Fourth paragraph (supporting detail)

Roller coasters are the most thrilling rides. You feel like you are flying. You feel scared when you drop down the hills. Everyone screams with excitement.

Last paragraph (conclusion)

Carousels just go around and around. Pirate ships swing back and forth. The tilt-a-whirl spins. Roller coasters do it all. Roller coasters rule!

23

Revising your writing is like adding more flavors of ice cream.

Adding Some Flavor: Revision

The walls may be up, but your ice cream shop is not ready to open. **Step 3: Revision** is the most important part of the writing process. Why isn't your draft perfect the first time? Writers are like everyone else—they make mistakes. You want your writing to be the best it can be. That usually means making some changes. Revision is adding words you need and taking away words you don't. You also move words around so they make sense. Revising is not just fixing a few little mistakes. You might make some major changes.

An ice cream shop would be no fun if it only had vanilla. It needs caramel swirl, peanut

Step 1: Prewriting

Step 2: Drafting

Step 3: Revision

Step 4: Peer Review

Step 5: Publishing

Do you need help adding flavor to your writing? Try to write a whole paragraph describing freshly baked chocolate chip cookies.

butter chip, and marshmallow mash! Your writing also needs more exciting "flavors." These flavors are details. They make your writing more interesting for a reader. Adding details also helps make your writing complete and understandable to the reader.

Pretend you are a reader of your piece instead of the writer. What parts seem to last too long? Do you repeat the same idea? You might want to fix these parts. Try to make them less wordy.

Now look for parts that seem rushed. For example, did you write only one sentence about a very important moment? Take some time to make the moment more exciting. Add descriptive details.

In creative writing, you create your own narrator and characters. The narrator is the person telling the story.

The characters are the people (or animals) in the story. Think about how they feel. Are they happy, scared, angry, or surprised? How can you show these feelings to your reader?

You can also add details by thinking about the five senses. Let's say you are writing about your favorite food. What does it taste, smell, and look like? How does it sound while it's cooking? How does it feel as you swallow it? These details make your topic more real to your readers.

Adding details can also spice up a character's personality. If you write "John smiled" or "Eileen smiled," we don't know much about John or Eileen. Now, look what happens when we add details:

John's mouth curled up at each end like a snake. We could see dirty teeth as jagged as rocks.
Eileen's mouth burst with a smile that lit up her face like fireworks.

This sentence could use more details:

Chocolate chip cookies are really delicious.

Here is a revised version of the same idea. It has details about feelings, senses, and mood.

My heart starts to pound when Mom takes the cookies out of the oven. Bumpy hills of oatmeal rise above melty lakes of chocolate. The rising steam hooks my nose and pulls me closer as I breathe the sweet air. I can't help snatching one cookie from the end. I take a bite. I feel the soft cookie in my mouth. Then I swallow, and the warmth spreads all the way down to my toes.

Another part of revision is making sure details are in the right sequence, or order. These sentences are in a confusing order:

All the lions of a pride eat together. They stuff themselves with zebra meat.

A lioness waits in the tall grass until just the right moment. Then she runs after a zebra, pulls it down, and kills it.

Lions are fierce predators. They can kill animals that are faster and bigger than they are.

Lions sometimes drag their prey to a shady spot.

Putting the sentences in a different sequence helps the reader put events in order:

Lions are fierce predators. They can kill animals that are faster and bigger than they are.

A lioness waits in the tall grass until just the right moment. Then she runs after a zebra, pulls it down, and kills it. Lions sometimes drag their prey to a shady spot.

All the lions of a pride eat together. They stuff themselves with zebra meat.

A lioness waits in the grass as she stalks her prey.

You can also use time words to put your facts in the right sequence:

First, we packed our beach bag.
Then we drove to the beach.
Next, we walked out on the sand.
Last, we huddled under the umbrella. It was raining!

The next step in revision is to look at your words and think about better ones. Make sure every word you choose has the right meaning. It should also set the mood you want for your piece. Mood is how you want your readers to feel.

First, look at nouns and see if you can be more specific.

Simon picked up his things.

When you revise, replace the word *things* with examples that tell us more about Simon:

Simon picked up his slingshot, paper clip collection, and teddy bear.

Now take a closer look at your verbs.

Susie jumps.

Jumps isn't a very exciting word. How about if Susie *springs* from her chair? Or she could *leap* to catch a falling glass dish.

Look at adjectives, too. You might want to use the word *good* or *happy*. But how about telling your reader even more? Say *massive* mountain instead of just *big* mountain. Don't just say you had a *fun* day. Say you had a *stupendous* day!

The last step of the revision process is checking for mistakes. This is called proofreading. First, check your punctuation. Do all of your sentences have periods, exclamation points, or question marks at the end? Did you use quotation marks (" ") when people are speaking? Did you indent a few spaces at the beginning of each paragraph?

In the Writing Tool Belt: The Flavorful Thesaurus

A thesaurus is a reference book for writers. A reference book gives you quick information. Many computers have thesauruses built in. You can find them on the Internet, too. In a thesaurus, you can look up a common word. Then you'll see other words with a similar meaning. This helps you come up with more exciting words. Here are some entries from an online thesaurus:

SCARY: alarming, chilling, creepy, eerie, spooky

HAPPY: cheerful, ecstatic, joyful, merry

BIG: bulky, grand, tall, roomy[2]

You can't just choose any word you want from the list. For example, *bulky* and *grand* don't mean exactly the same thing! Use the word that best fits your meaning.

Check spelling, too. Make sure to have a dictionary nearby. If you are not sure how something is spelled, look it up. If you wrote your piece on a computer, use the spell checker. Proceed with caution, though! You still need to read through your whole piece. Double-check for spelling mistakes. You might have mixed up *there* and *their*. The spell checker won't catch it.

Finally, check your grammar. (See Chapter 6.) Make sure you use the right form of the verb with your subject. For example, one balloon *floats*, but two balloons *float*. Also make sure you use the right verb tenses. The goldfish *swam* yesterday, but he *swims* today.

Your ice cream shop is almost ready for business!

In the Writing Tool Belt: The All-Knowing Dictionary

A dictionary doesn't just tell you how to spell a word. It also tells you the part of speech and how to pronounce the word. It provides all of the word's meanings. Some dictionaries even tell you what language the word comes from.

Chapter

4

Getting an Inspection: Peer Review

Once a store has been built, an inspector comes in. The inspector makes sure everything works. You need an inspector for your writing, too. We have reached **Step 4: Peer Review**. Your peer reviewer gives you feedback. He or she can suggest ways to make your piece better.

Peer review is when you get opinions and advice from a writing partner. Your partner could be a friend or a classmate. Your partner might use a form with places to fill in, such as "My favorite part was . . ." or "I think you can make it better by . . ."

Step 1: Prewriting

Step 2: Drafting

Step 3: Revision

Step 4: Peer Review

Step 5: Publishing

If your teacher gave you a rubric, your partner might use it during peer review. Here is an example of a rubric:

❑ Was the main idea clear?

❑ Did the writer give at least three supporting details?

❑ Are all words spelled correctly?

❑ Is punctuation in the right place?

Writers don't have to do all the work by themselves! Try working with a peer review partner.

A good peer reviewer gives you helpful feedback. It is not helpful to say, "I didn't like the beginning because it was boring." Here is some helpful feedback: "The beginning didn't tell me very much. I wanted to know more about the spaceship."

Professional Inspectors

At a publishing company, an editor is like a teacher. He or she reads an author's manuscript and makes suggestions for improvement. An editor is also like a peer review partner. Authors and editors work as a team to make a piece of writing the best it can be.

Your partner has given you feedback. What should you do with it? Think about what your partner liked or didn't like. Decide if you want to make some changes. Then get back to work and fix it.

You can do a peer review anytime. You don't have to wait until you are finished writing. Ask a friend for help during the prewriting, drafting, and revision steps, too.

When your writing is finished, open for business and share it with the world!

Time to Share! Publishing

Your ice cream shop has passed inspection. Now it's ready to open for business! How do you know when you are ready to "open for business" and share your writing? That is for you to decide. Are you happy with what you have created? It's never too late to fix and revise. If you're ready, it's time for **Step 5: Publishing**.

Open the door to your ice cream shop, and invite in some customers. Let them enjoy what you've built. That's what publishing is like. Publishing is when an author shares his or her work with a larger audience. The writing might turn into a book, a

Step 1: Prewriting

Step 2: Drafting

Step 3: Revision

Step 4: Peer Review

Step 5: Publishing

37

magazine article, or a Web site. You can publish your writing, too.

Start by reading your piece aloud to your class or to your family. This is one way to share it. You could create your own greeting card with a poem that you wrote. You could write down family memories in a scrapbook. You could post your article on a Web site or a blog.

Or how about making your own book? All you need is nice paper and a stapler or ribbon! Many writers keep everything they have written. It's fun to look back and see how you have grown as a writer.

Your hard work was worth it. Now everyone can enjoy the writing you built with your ideas!

Making your own book is a fun way to publish your writing.

38

Grammar and Punctuation Guide

Here are the parts of speech you need to build your piece of writing.

Noun—a person, place, or thing. Nouns can be singular (one) or plural (more than one). You can usually make a noun plural by adding -s or -es—but not always. Check a dictionary if you are unsure about how to spell a plural noun.

Singular	Plural
jellybean	jellybeans
child	children
fish	fish

Proper nouns refer to specific people, places, or things, such as *Mississippi, George Washington,* and *Amazon River.* The first letter of a proper noun is capitalized.

Common nouns refer to general people, places, or things, such as *students, school,* and *popcorn.*

39

Pronoun—a word that takes the place of a noun, such as *he, she, it,* and *they.*

Possessive pronouns show ownership. They include *his, hers, its,* and *their.*

Verb—a word that shows action or state of being.

Words such as *jump, read,* and *cry* are action verbs.

To be, to feel, and *to seem* are states of being. For example, you can *be* hungry, *feel* nervous, or *seem* unhappy.

The tense of a verb shows when the action takes place. Present tense means it is happening right now. Past tense means it happened in the past. Simple future tense means it will happen in the future.

Regular verbs don't change much in each tense.

Maya loves hot dogs. (present tense)

Maya loved hot dogs. (past tense)

Maya will love hot dogs. (simple future tense)

Irregular verbs have a different form in past tense.

Maya eats ten hot dogs. (present tense)

Maya ate ten hot dogs. (past tense)

Maya will eat ten hot dogs. (simple future tense)

The verb *to be* also changes form in different tenses.

Maya is very full. (present tense)

Maya was very full. (past tense)

Maya will be very full. (simple future tense)

Adjective—a word that tells more about a noun. Adjectives are descriptive words, such as *lovely, yellow,* and *silly.* A noun can have more than one adjective:

the <u>round</u>, <u>sticky</u>, <u>red</u> <u>peppermint</u> candy

Adverb—a word that tells more about a verb, adjective, or other adverb. Adverbs often answer the questions How? When? Why? or How much?

Red Riding Hood skipped <u>merrily</u> to Grandma's house. (tells more about the verb *skipped*)

We are <u>very</u> confused about the homework. (tells more about the adjective *confused*)

Preposition—a word that connects one word to another word or phrase. It often tells where something is or where it goes. Examples are *over, between, of, to, on,* and *with.* The preposition and the words following it are called a **prepositional phrase.**

George jumped <u>over the rock</u>.

Conjunction—a word that links words, phrases, or clauses in a sentence, such as *and, but, or,* and *so.*

The dog has fangs, <u>so</u> Chris never runs past its house.

Interjection—a word or words that express emotion. An interjection can be followed by a comma or an exclamation point, depending on how strong the emotion is.

Well, *I guess you can borrow my favorite sweater.*

Yikes! *You spilled grape juice all over it.*

Keep this grammar guide close by as you proofread your writing. Your teacher—and your readers—will appreciate it!

The parts of speech can be put together in many different ways.

Phrase—a group of words with a single meaning. A phrase doesn't have a subject and verb. All the words together can act as a part of speech.

The boy with the big hat looks ridiculous. ("with the big hat" acts as an adjective describing the boy)

The two girls laughed at the same time. ("at the same time" acts as an adverb telling when the girls were laughing)

Clause—a group of words that has a subject and verb and can act as a part of speech.

Independent clauses can stand alone as a sentence or be a part of a bigger sentence.

Jacob plays baseball with his father every day of the week. ("Jacob plays baseball" is an independent clause with a subject and verb)

Dependent (subordinate) clauses cannot stand alone as a sentence and must be part of a bigger sentence.

Emily uses markers when she draws pictures. ("when she draws pictures" is a dependent clause)

Sentences often combine the two types of clauses.

I can't decide whether I like chocolate more than lollipops. The first part of the sentence can stand on its own (independent clause). The second part cannot (dependent clause).

Your sentences need punctuation. Punctuation marks help your writing make sense and tell your reader how your words should be read.

Punctuation Rules

* Capitalize the first letter of a sentence, and put a period at the end.
* Replace the period with a question mark if the sentence is a question.
* Replace the period with an exclamation point if you want to show strong feeling.
* Put commas between words in lists, between clauses, and to set one thought apart from another.
* Put quotation marks around sentences that are spoken by a character.
* Use apostrophes to show possession (*Dana's book*) or to make contractions (*is not → isn't*).

Your nouns and verbs have to agree. That means they make sense together.

Noun-Verb Agreement

When a noun is singular, the verb often ends in *-s.*
The <u>*cat purrs*</u> *all day.*
When the noun is plural, the verb usually does not end in *-s.*
The <u>*cats purr*</u> *all day.*
The verb *to be* changes depending on the subject.
I <u>*am*</u> *happy.*
You <u>*are*</u> *happy.*
He <u>*is*</u> *happy.*
They <u>*are*</u> *happy.*

Glossary

blueprint—A plan for creating something.

brainstorming—Writing down everything that comes into your head about a particular topic.

compound sentence—Two sentences linked with a conjunction to make one sentence.

conclusion—A sentence or paragraph that summarizes a piece of writing.

creative writing—Writing with the main purpose of entertaining the reader.

direct object—A person or thing that the action of a verb is done *to*.

drafting—Using your prewriting plan to write a full version of your piece.

expository writing—Writing meant to share information or to teach the reader.

feedback—Someone else's opinions or thoughts about your work.

graphic organizers—Charts, diagrams, or other ways to organize your thoughts during prewriting.

indirect object—A person or thing an action is being done *for* or *to*.

introduction—The first part of a piece of writing; it states your main idea and describes your topic.

main idea—What your writing is about.

mood—The feeling that an author wants to give his or her readers.

peer review—Sharing your work with other writers to gather feedback.

plagiarism—Using someone else's work as your own without giving credit to the source of the work.

predicate—The part of a sentence that includes the verb; it describes what the subject is doing or feeling.

prewriting—Organizing your thoughts to prepare for writing. This includes brainstorming, using graphic organizers, and creating a writing plan.

process—Something that happens over time, in a series of steps.

proofreading—Reading your piece to find spelling, grammar, and punctuation mistakes.

publishing—Sharing your completed work with a larger audience.

reference book—A book full of quick facts, such as a dictionary or thesaurus.

revision—Adding, taking away, or reorganizing words to improve your piece of writing.

rubric—A list of what a teacher expects a piece of writing to include.

sequence—The order of events in a piece of writing.

subject—The noun or pronoun that tells who or what the sentence is about.

thesaurus—A reference book or computer tool with entries that list a word along with other words that have the same or similar meaning.

Chapter Notes

1. Personal interview with Christie Wall, March 25, 2008.

2. Dictionary.com, LLC, *Thesaurus.com*, n.d., <www.thesaurus.com> (June 15, 2008).

Further Reading

Books

Cleary, Brian P. *I and You and Don't Forget Who: What Is a Pronoun?* Minneapolis, Minn.: First Avenue Editions, 2006.

Leedy, Loreen. *Look at My Book: How Kids Can Write and Illustrate Terrific Books.* New York: Holiday House, 2005.

Rhatigan, Joe. *Write Now!: The Ultimate, Grab-a-Pen, Get-the-Words-Right, Have-a-Blast Writing Book.* New York: Lark Books, 2005.

TIME for Kids Magazine Editors. *Ready, Set, Write! A Writer's Handbook for School and Home.* New York: Time for Kids, 2006.

Truss, Lynne. *Twenty-Odd Ducks: Why, Every Punctuation Mark Counts!* New York: G. P. Putnam's Sons, 2008.

On the Internet

Education Place Graphic Organizers
http://www.eduplace.com/graphicorganizer/

Internet Public Library: KidSpace
http://www.ipl.org/div/kidspace/

Wow! Grammar: How to Master Skills to Succeed
http://www.scholastic.com/kids/homework/grammar.htm

Index